Toward Revitalization

9 ORDERLY STEPS TO CHURCH HEALTH

Dr. Brian E Nall

ISBN-13: 978-0-578-45101-5

Published by Brian E Nall
Pensacola, FL

To the churches of the Pensacola Bay Baptist Association, aspiring to be healthy churches working together for the glory of God.

To Baleigh and Elijah, the best children a dad could have

To Candace, my forever beautiful bride

CONTENTS

ACKNOWLEDGMENTS

A new and exciting day is emerging in Associational life within the Southern Baptist Convention. Across the country churches are gaining a renewed appreciation for working together for the Kingdom. As an Associational Mission Strategist[1], I have the privilege of working with a great group of pastors and churches across Escambia County, Florida. Your support and encouragement is a great gift to me.

Thank you to Corina Lavenberg, PBBA Ministry Assistant, for your tireless work to serve churches and to help this book become a reality. You have routinely answered the call to serve Christ among the nations, and your servant's heart is now impacting 1000's across the PBBA.

Thank you Lewis Miller, Florida Baptist Convention West Region Catalyst. You have lived out well the convention tagline of "Right Beside You" by being boots on the ground here in the Panhandle.

[1] This is the new title for the Director of a Southern Baptist Convention Association, formerly Director of Missions, was adopted in 2018. At the time of this book's writing my official title is Executive Director.

Introduction

PREPARING TO STEP

What's first? What's next? Sounds like simple enough questions but all too often these questions are neglected to be asked and answered within church ministry. In general, the question falls to "What must we do?" If not careful, a pile of the "must do" on the church calendar and emergencies of the moment will fill our day only to see that little has changed within church health or Kingdom advance. Frustration is still high. Holy outcomes are still low.

In Luke 14 Jesus is unfolding what following Him will entail. For those who want to rush forward with focused faith, Jesus gives them reason to pause and consider before they run to act.

> *"[27]Whoever does not carry his own cross and come after Me cannot be My disciple. [28]For which one of you, when he wants to build a tower, does not first sit down and calculate the cost to see if he has enough to complete it? [29]Otherwise, when he has laid a foundation and is not able to finish, all who observe it begin to ridicule him, [30]saying, 'This man began to build and was not able to finish.'"* - *Luke 14*

Jesus is clear, there is expectation in following Jesus. There are terms. His terms. Consequently, you have to count the cost. Like a builder, planning is required. Cost must be considered. If you are going to get where you want to get, *think* about it. Such calculation and forethought is essential for being a healthy church.

This book is designed to help churches think about order. In order for us to be biblically healthy and obedient to what God has called each church to, "What's first? What's next?"

Before you get into paragraph one, don't assume these steps toward revitalization are some magical formula. This process will be a flop if not rooted in prayer. Further, the answers to the presented questions will not be the same for each church. While we must all stand as the church of Jesus Christ under the immovable and unalterable word of God, we have been divinely placed in unique contexts. Jesus continues to hold the responsibility to build HIS church; but at the same time He has entrusted to us the privilege of operating appropriately within His body, wherever in the world that may be.

I encourage you to read this book with a group of your church leaders. You will get the most benefit out of the questions by answering them within the context of a community. Further, such group work will hold you accountable to face the answer to the potentially really hard question. Additionally, working toward revitalization *together* will foster a shared journey for your church instead of the efforts of the church leader hoping to pull everyone else along at a later time. Hold on. First will come some pain, but then will come the journey. The journey *toward revitalization.*

CHAPTER 1

HOW DID WE GET HERE?

"Those who don't learn from the past are doomed to repeat it."

-George Santayana

On occasion while our family is eating dinner at our kitchen table, one of the kids will accidentally knock over their drink. Next, as the spilt drink is running across the table and onto the floor, they look at me. At that point I usually remark, "Don't just sit there, clean it up. Looking at a problem won't fix it." (As you are imagining this scene, please picture me saying this calmly and in an encouraging tone.) I admit that my frustration grows when anyone only wants to *inspect* a problem but gives little effort to flinch a muscle to *fix* it. But inspecting the problem does have its place and is helpful.

In church revitalization, there can be an urgency to clean up the "spill" of unhealth as fast as possible. Perhaps you are speed-reading through this book for that very purpose. It doesn't feel good to roll around in the swamp of messy church. Thus, a church seeking to experience revitalization and sustained health can shift into high gear so that they can get out of their mess. That move can be admirable; but if they do not spend some time identifying how they ended up where they did, they might set a course for their church that just gets them stuck again. They speed off in the wrong direction doing the wrong thing, only faster. They get out of one sand trap and into a water hazard (I don't play golf, so I hope you are impressed with the analogy). Church messes that sound the call for revitalization can be categorized by both the kind of decline and by the speed of decline. Let's look at both.

Kind of Decline

Attendance

Attendance is generally the most common statistic churches keep track of (remember the brown attendance board up next to the choir loft). The math of tracking attendance ends up being closely connected to emotions. When the sum total goes up, smiles go up; when the sum total goes down, people frown.

Baptism

Baptisms, or rather the lack thereof, can be a key indicator of concern. While a church cannot control salvations, they can control, or at least greatly influence, the number of gospel conversations their people have and how they are engaging the spiritually lost world around them. Generally (there are exceptions), the more a church is "being a witness," the more people who will entrust their heart to Christ and, in turn, the more the baptismal waters will be stirred. Now, if there is a one-year slump, okay; but if there are multiple years of decline or no baptisms, red flags should begin to be raised.

Volunteerism/Service

The level of volunteerism can indicate how much people "buy-in" to what is happening at your church. This level is best calculated by a percentage and not by a number. As such, if there is a declining percentage of people who are serving, that can indicate a growing percentage of spectators and/or people who are not willing to help move the church forward in the preferred direction. Also, if those who are serving have been doing it so long so that they are physically unable to serve any longer and there are not new people coming in who are able to fill those gaps or continue a God-given ministry for another generation, your level of concern should also grow.

Giving

"Where your treasure is, there your heart will be also" (Matthew 6:21). Thereby, if people in your church are choosing, in growing measure, to direct their

"treasures" elsewhere, that can be a sign that their heart is elsewhere. Now, is financial stewardship a matter of discipleship? Definitely. Scripture is clear that we are to bring our tithes into the storehouse of the local church regardless of one's emotions in the moment or in a frustrating season.[2] We give *to God.* But many people will lead their lives through the wallet. A decline in giving can be an indicator there is a low level of trust in church leadership, or at least a lack of confidence. While God's people are to give *to God*, they give *through* the local church. And if they don't trust the conduit; they tend to redirect their giving elsewhere. Further, if you can trace a steady decline in giving, that can also indicate a steady decline in givers. It might be a good idea to work with your church treasurer or finance team to identify the number people in your church who have given in the past in order to identify any trends – more people giving or less.

Spiritual Growth

[2] Malachi 3:10

This kind of decline can be the most difficult to detect. It is connected to heart. It is "soul data." You could take church health surveys via the *Transformational Church Assessment Toolkit* from Lifeway (TCAT)[3], but they still only scratch the surface. But hearts *do* reveal themselves ("out of the mouth the heart speaks", Matthew 12:34). Consequently, unrighteous anger dominates business meetings. Personal preferences shout down biblical mandates. Unholy and spiritually immature suggestions are frequent in committee meetings. Social media becomes the primary way to deal with church issues. Gossip grows rapidly in activity and in approval. You easily identify which church (or churches) you reflect from the seven of Revelation. Therefore, if the trend of conversation is moving away from holiness, warning bells should begin to go off.

Connection to Community

---

[3] The Transformational Church Assessment Tool (TCAT) provides your church with the ability to assess the health of the congregation, celebrate areas of strength, and address areas of concern. The TCAT is available at https://tcat.lifeway.com

Your church is not haphazardly located. It is in a unique community. Because of its location and the accompanying mandate for the church to be a witness (I like to call them "ambassadors of heaven"), those who surround the gathering place of the church should be affected by its presence and activity. But if your community doesn't notice your church, that should be concerning. If the *value* of your property is of more interest than your *influence* in the community, that too should be concerning. When taking a new pastorate, I walked the surrounding neighborhood doing survey work for the church. Asking one neighbor what they thought of my new church, she couldn't give an answer because she had never really noticed it before – even though it was only a few hundred yards away.

Do communities change? Most definitely. But it is a mandate of the church to continually adjust their methodology accordingly while holding steadfast to their theology. If this doesn't happen, and the community and church grow in their disparity, the church risks turning into an island and circling the wagons, cutting itself off from its Great Commission mission.

Speed of Decline

Sudden (Under 2 years)

When sudden negative change occurs in a church, everyone knows. It is something that just cannot be kept quiet or swept under the rug. "Sudden" situations often occur when there has been a moral failure by the leadership or some major divisiveness that has led to some sort of mass exodus of people. The "sudden" examples often make their way to the news media, but most often are widely known throughout the community, both inside and outside church circles. Consequently, attendance is lower, the baptistry develops cobwebs, volunteers resign, giving plummets, spiritual growth is often overtaken by anger and antagonists, and the community looks at the church with great animosity.

Slow (2-9 years)

Slow decline does not see the visible impact as does "sudden" decline, but there is an underlying unsettledness among the people that something is not normal. Slow declines can arise at times of transition in leadership or extended change in a community. Some percentage of the people become unsatisfied with church leadership and they slowly trickle away to other churches or, sadly, just stay home. Businesses relocate or military bases close; and while people try to hang around as long as possible, people begin to drift away. Consequently, it doesn't take much effort to list those who have strolled out the doors of the church over the past decade and, without giving much or any explanation, have not returned.

Deceptive (10+ years)

Deceptive decline is the most difficult to identify; hence, "deceptive." When deceptive decline occurs in a church, the majority don't notice, perhaps really don't care. For instance, a church declines in attendance by 1-2% each year for 15 years. When observing year to year, the change doesn't feel that big.

Moving from an average of 140 to 138 doesn't induce panic. No one really feels or sees the pain. But if you were to compare a trend over the whole 15 years, there would be a decline of 15-30% (98 instead of 140 using the previous example). That is big. Further, if the weekly, monthly, or annual budget is mostly being met and those who remain are still able to have many of the activities they enjoy, the decline can be even more deceptively hidden. Consequently, the average age of the church can diverge from the average age of the surrounding community; and the community can merely view the church as a non-factor, even blind to its presence.

Mess Analysis

Where you are as a church is most likely a combination of the descriptions above. I realize that some decline, in both kind and speed, can be the result of leaders making a needed decision but not everyone agreeing. But let me encourage you not to assume this by your own analysis and assumptions. "Be quick to listen, slow to speak, and slow to become angry"

(James 1:19). Do the hard work of finding out what is truly going on – the good, the bad and the ugly.

Toward Reflection

1) Do you see a decline in your church?
2) If so, what is the nature of the decline – Attendance? Giving? Serving? Spiritual? Combination? All of the above? If so, what is the speed? Is it sudden, slow, or deceptive?
3) After identifying the nature and speed of your decline, do you have a handle on "why?" Consider speaking with a couple of trusted individuals to help you identify the "why".

CHAPTER 2

STEP 1| PRAYER

'My house will be called a house of prayer'

– Jesus

When Neil Armstrong was about to make his "one small step for man" stride onto the surface of the moon, he wasn't 100% sure what he was getting into. Would his foot sink deep or only make an imprint? The whole "the first step could be a doozy" was an understatement. Fortunately, his uncertainty didn't paralyze him on the bottom rung of the ladder. That might have made the blooper reels for a long time.

As with moon landings, when moving toward revitalization, the first step *is crucial.* When your church finds herself at the "bottom," either suddenly, slowly or deceptively, there is only one way to go – up[4]. But how do you move in that preferred upward healthy trajectory? How do you actually stand victoriously on the other side of a goal you previously saw as a far-fetched? Such feelings of being on the bottom can seem dire, and you can be tempted to reach out to grasp at anything that moves which could lend you a hand. Searching Google for solutions. Creating Facebook polls. Researching Wikipedia "wisdom." Attending yet *another* conference. I get it. I got that t-shirt too. But is your church missing the most basic atom of our faith?

What about prayer?

Prayer all too often crosses our mind *after* we have done all the heavy-lifting work and then lift our plans for God to bless. And if feeling a bit more spiritual, we

---

[4] without digging a grave and closing the doors.

open a planning meeting in routine prayer before we get to the typed agenda before us. But I contend, may I say *strongly* contend, that establishing a prayer strategy up front, actually a prayer *culture*, will lay the best groundwork and serve as the best first step for moving your church toward revitalization.

Creating a prayer strategy/culture is rooted in the clear teachings of Jesus – whom we say we follow and are His ambassadors[5] and are to function as reflections of Christ, hence "Christian."

- "My house shall be called a house of prayer" (Matthew 21:13).
- "The prayer of a righteous man is powerful and effective" (James 5:16).
- "Therefore I want the men in every place to pray, lifting up holy hands, without wrath and dissension" (1 Timothy 2:8).

When we read such passages, we "Amen" and heartily approve with public pronouncements. But all too often our personal practice does not reflect those

[5] 2 Corinthians 5:1-18

public pronouncements. Prayer is not to merely be the last response to our planning efforts or the formal opening to our meeting formalities; rather, God has given prayer as a privileged resource to serve as the pencil we first pick up to draw with in order to craft our ministry blueprints. Through prayer God's power is ignited, His peace is enjoyed, His guidance is instilled, His timing is experienced, His presence is realized. Conversely, if prayer is not *actually practiced* within the church (and I don't mean having dedicated time to take prayer requests and then print a list), then God's power, peace, guidance, timing and presence will be replaced by the efforts and resources His finite and fallen children can muster. Resources will be wasted. Effort will be unnecessarily expended or misused. The Kingdom will be minimally expanded. And all will be frustrated. It is for this reason that prayer is the first step for any church moving toward revitalization. But how?

Personal

Being a praying church begins with you, the pastor, church leader, or ministry team. The old adage goes, "your people will not go further than their leader." Thus, it is imperative that you become a praying person. I don't mean faithfully asking God to bless the food or turning church announcements into a prayer format – "Lord, please help everyone come this afternoon at 4:30 p.m. to the dinner, bring side dishes to go with the meat the church provides, invite a guest and use the side door next to the Fellowship Hall." (Can you tell this is a pet peeve of mine?) Rather, a person of prayer is one who is familiar with approaching the throne of grace[6] and talks to the Lord like Moses, walks with Him like Enoch, shows his face to God like Moses, while loving him like David. Perhaps you would not check the "prayer warrior" box on a survey. May I ask that you begin.

Fortunately, the Holy Spirit is able to take our self-perceived inadequacies in prayer, even groans[7], and present them to the Father. But you have to begin. You have to choose to bend the knee and begin to

[6] Hebrews 4:16
[7] Romans 8:26

pray. If reading a book on prayer (like E.M. Bounds collection of small books on prayer[8], or Ronnie Floyd's "The Power of Prayer and Fasting,"[9] or H.B. Charles's great book on preaching and prayer "It Happens After Prayer"[10]) or listening to a sermon series (like the testimony of Jim Cymbala from Brooklyn Tabernacle[11]) will help you get kickstarted, fine. But the best format is just to begin. And begin *simply.*

- "Lord, help."
- "Jesus, what's the next thing I must do, I must *be*, to lead and shepherd YOUR church?"
- "What must change in me so that I can be the person You desire me to be?
- "Jesus, thank you for blessing me. How can I bless You today?
- "Lord, I humbly ask for wisdom to lead Your church."

[8] Bounds, E.M., *The Complete Work of E.M. Bounds*, (Michigan: Baker Books, 1990).
[9] Floyd, Ronnie, *The Power of Prayer and Fasting*, (Nashville: B&H Publishing, 2010).
[10] Charles, H.B., *It Happens After Prayer*, (Chicago: Moody Publishing, 2013).
[11] Available at https://www.youtube.com/watch?v=40F5wMbjugE

And then, quiet yourself even more and listen. Listen through reading His word. Write down what God is showing you through His word. Listen. And as you take one step at a time, God will continue to show you the next step. But He won't show you the *next* step until you are willing to take the *first* step. It's like headlights on a car- you walk in the light of what He shows you and then He will shine even farther down the road. But remember, God is more interested in *you and your people and your community* than in any program you begin or an event your church hosts. He didn't die for a strategy. He died for you and wants to know you. He's not as interested in your ability to translate a text or plan a smooth event as He is in your willingness to hear His still small voice.

"Lord, your servant here. I'm listening."

Prayer Team

Being a *person* of prayer (singular) is good but being *people* of prayer (plural) is even better. Remember, when two or three people gather in God's name, He is in their midst.[12] Thus, there is tremendous power when people gather to pray. Now, I get that hosting a church-wide prayer gathering doesn't usually call for extra chairs to be on the ready. Prayer is a battle and many people, while being fans of prayer, are not fiercely willing to adjust their schedule to be on bended knee to push forward God's purposes and push back the darkness. They don't wield the weapon of prayer routinely.[13] But just because the masses don't rush to join you in prayer doesn't call for you to dismiss prayer as your first steps toward revitalization. Obeying God's word, being a house of prayer, should not be contingent on what is popular. Faithful biblical leaders don't take a poll of the people and then lead accordingly; they lead biblically, regardless. Remember, God's ways are not our ways, and our churches will be healthiest over the long term when we follow His blueprint. Pray!

How?

---

[12] Matthew 18:20

[13] On a side note: I contend that the primary reason America is experiencing so little a move of God is directly connected to so little prayer in Christian churches.

Select two to three people who you know are people of prayer (even one person if that is all you got). Ask them to join you to pray. Perhaps you decide that a Saturday evening, Sunday morning or other time will be best. Great! Just get going. Begin by praying over your church campus, prayer-walking through each room, even the parking lot. Pray over the doorways that members and guests will pass through. Pray over each family by systematically going over a membership roll or a pictorial directory.

A great strategy is from Pastor Steve Gaines of Bellevue Baptist Church in Memphis, the three-month multiplication prayer plan. Get three people to join you thirty minutes before your Sunday morning schedule begins. If Small Groups begin at 9:30 a.m., then begin at 9:00 a.m. The three of you are to pray over each spot in your worship center: each pew, the pulpit, the choir, the soundboard, the entry doors, the whole thing. Perhaps even walk through the building turning on lights and praying over each room, each chair. However you decide, the three of you pray for thirty minutes, each Sunday for three months. After those three months, each of you are to invite one additional person to join you. That will result in six people praying for thirty minutes over your campus. After another three months, the six are to each invite another person – we are now at twelve. If you do the math, this will result in twenty-four people praying by the time you wrap up the first year and exponentially more people in following years (I dare you to calculate the number for how many would be praying at the end of year three).

What to pray?

- For Humility to mark your demeanor.
- For Revival to begin in your hearts.
- For Repentance to define your day.
- For God to move – convict, stir, empower, heal, restore.
- For sinners to be saved, for marriages to be restored, for the pastor to be empowered.
- For God to be glorified.

Remember, "you have not because you ask not."

Additional Tip

Begin to celebrate prayer in your worship services. I encourage you to install a "God Answers Prayer" board in or by your worship center. Then, take the prayer requests people submit each week and have them stamp it "prayer answered" when you hear of their request being answered. Collect all the answered prayers on the board as a testimony to the work of God. Remember, people will gravitate to what you celebrate.

Toward Reflection

1. Would I consider myself a person of prayer? If not, what can I do to begin? What time will I set aside? Who could I contact to help me?
2. What could we add (or even take away) so that prayer becomes central to our church? Who else do I need to speak with in the church to help me take this first step of prayer?

Toward Revitalization: Where you Are

Prayerful
Biblical
Categorical
Contextual
Directional
Organizational
Functional
Communicative
Evaluative

CHAPTER 3

STEP 2| BIBLICAL

"Thy Word is a Lamp Unto My Feet and a Light Unto they Path"
-Psalms 119:105

My son Elijah is a fan of all things Disney. While he definitely enjoys when our family goes to one of the theme parks, he also enjoys studying how the Disney company works. Beginning when he was ten, Elijah would listen to the Disney podcast "WDW." Those podcasts would reveal the "how" behind the Disney magic "what." His inquisitive mind soaked it up. On more than one occasion Elijah would walk into the room and inform us of the wait time for various rides in Disney World: Jungle Cruise, 45 minutes; Peter Pan Ride, 100 minutes; Mine Train, 220 minutes. How did he know that? Answer – he downloaded the WDW app. Through the app, maps and tips were there at his fingertips. If we had been in the park, we could leverage that information to more effectively navigate our way through the masses (and with a possible 220+ minute wait time that is a bunch of "masses"). Thus, we had no excuse to wander aimlessly. No reason why we could not maximize every minute. Fortunately, God has given churches an "app" to help them be healthy and to move toward revitalization – His Word, the Bible.

As you begin to get your prayer legs under you (Chapter 2), the next step toward revitalization lies in tangibly and practically embracing God's word. Such an embrace requires a church to move past solely *understanding* the Bible as its chief purpose and, instead, be resolved toward *application*. As the Bible is a "lamp unto our feet and light unto our path" (Psalm 119:105), its effectiveness depends on our walking in it through every stride we take and not merely developing programming or events to study its packaging. Imagine the foolishness of someone only studying the package of a flashlight but never actually turning it on and using it. Sadly, this description fits all too many churches. They proclaim the Bible but never tangibly lead to weave it into their practice. They compartmentalize the Bible - proclaiming it in a sermon but not transferring the application of the sermon onto the church calendar. Many a church leaders have sought catchy phrases to define the steps they will take toward health yet they are void of biblical roots. Consequently, they have wandered aimlessly, never reaching their preferred future. But as "people of the Book" our theology must be the primary source that fuels our methodology. The Bible must be formed into our routine practices, not just proclaimed as public principles. Even in a day when our culture is driven by entertainment, mass media, and emoji-based communication, following the road map of the Bible remains fully sufficient.

How?

Transforming You

As mentioned previously, people will go no further than their leader. Thus, your personal time in the Bible is paramount and cannot be overemphasized. But your time in the Bible is not for mere personal information, rather for personal transformation. It is more important for the Bible to read you than for you to read the Bible. Every time you read God's word, you should learn something about God; and in so doing, learn something about yourself that needs to change so as to reflect more the character of Jesus. This is the life-long journey of sanctification. The process of moving information to transformation is a skill, a skill that you must develop. And a non-negotiable skill that your church must develop if it wants to move toward revitalization. Thankfully we have the Holy Spirit to empower us along that journey. But hear me clearly: if you choose *not* to partake of the process that moves biblical information to application and you choose instead to settle for only growing in mentally understanding the Bible (how many Bible verses can I memorize instead of what verses do I know that I must do), don't expect to see transformation occur within you or within your church. You and your congregants might win Bible drills and theology-bees (do they have that?), but the mission field of your community will be unaffected. Your sermons, and all of your ministry really, should inform the listener mentally; but your life lived of biblical application must be an equally loud sermon.

Transforming others

Sixty-six books; 31,102 verses. The wisdom of the Bible, the spiritual data, is massive. Fortunately, there is little room to go wrong when setting a biblical course for your church when coupled with an authentic prayer life and pursued within a community of other Christ followers.

To begin, prayerfully search the Bible for scriptural pillars that present a clear basis of following

Jesus. This will become the basis of the church. For instance, the end of 1 Corinthians 13 states "Faith, Hope and Love, but the greatest of these is love." Jesus gives additional truths that set up additional pillars - the Great Commandment and the Great Commission, for example. Additionally, Hebrews 12 outlines several "let us" statements for how the church is to do life as followers of Jesus. Ephesians 4 outlines the nature of both vertical and horizontal relationships. There are many others. To discover these, read the Bible together as church leaders. Pray. Make a list. After you have your list, again this could be ten or more passages, spend some time in prayer lifting up a simple prayer,

> *"Lord, we want to lead Your church to love all of Your word and be transformed by it. Would You show us which verse or passage would best be an understandable foundation for us to lead Your people who are in this church?"*

Time and again, I have seen the Holy Spirit begin to shrink that list. This "shrinking" is not discounting scripture as one having more eternal value than another; rather, emphasizing certain passages for a *particular* people, for such a time as now. Like building a home, all the pieces are used but some pieces can serve better as a foundation. Still other materials are good for the exterior while others are better for the interior. Some materials are better served in one climate than another. Consequently, your list of ten verses/passages is reduced to four or five.

At this point, begin to do a lot more homework. Take each of those passages and exegete them. Look at their context. Examine the original language. Read commentaries. Dig in. Bounce them off several wise advisors. As you work the passages, there will be some that hit closer to home than others. This is evidence that the Holy Spirit is working right along-side of you. Listen to His promptings. For instance, there will be a particular passage that seems to connect more to *your* people and the DNA of *your* church which is set in *your* community's context as compared to another (blindly copying the decisions of other churches won't do).

After your season of prayer and study and prioritizing, you should be down to one or two primary passages. I recommend no more than three key passages. From personal experience in this process, I have found there is an unexplainable peace when I get to those final scriptures, an internal release. Not because I am done with the difficult work, but more the feeling that the Holy Spirit has just signed off on a bit of the blueprint and it all peacefully "clicks".

This final passage, or perhaps passages, will become the public mission of your church - why we exist or, using secular slang, "what's business?". Thus, when your congregants are seeking to give an answer to their neighbor as to what their church is about, this passage will serve as a common foundation for them to shape the conversation around, a biblical foundation to succinctly have an "elevator conversation" with a curious friend. No more answers of, "I dunno, just cause." No more working away mindless routine religiosity just to see what pops out. (Can you imagine a restaurant that operated by that philosophy?). The amount of individualistic self-centered answers will be reduced because you have equipped your people with a biblical foundation.

Now that you have your foundational verses or passages, you cannot shelf them. In the coming chapters you will discover how to bring them into the everyday habits of your leadership. They will serve as a framework for your budget, for staffing, for calendaring, for components in your worship gatherings, even for casting a vision for your facility usage.

Toward Reflection

1. What changes in your study of the Bible need to occur so that there is more transformation as opposed to solely information?
2. What are ten primary scriptures that really stick out to you which seem to be pillars of Christianity and could serve to be pillars of your church?
3. How will you prayerfully work through your list to identify the ultimate biblical pillars of your church? Who needs to assist you in this process?

Toward Revitalization: Where you Are

Prayerful

Biblical

Categorical

Contextual

Directional

Organizational

Functional

Communicative

Evaluative

CHAPTER 4

STEP 3 | CATEGORICAL

"Be doers of the word and not hearers only"

– James 1:22

I'm not a fan of shopping. On most days I would rather do just about anything other than navigate crowds and racks of merchandise. However, there are some moments when I must suck it up, charge headlong into the faith-threatening experience and shop. And I do my best to grin and bear it (Candace says I pout when shopping, but that is only when in public). Every time I venture into the horrors of the shopping experience, I always have a list. My goal is to move as rapidly as I can from item to item so that I can get in and get out. I prefer to gage the quality of shopping based on the *time* I saved instead of the money I saved. As I am driving to the store, I often visualize the layout ahead of time so that I can move most efficiently through the store, even including where I park if there are multiple entrances.

Having the items placed in their proper categories, or departments depending on the store, eases the pain and makes shopping tolerable (I am not yet to the point where I can write "enjoyable."). There are other stores I have entered where there are no categories or departments, and it looked more like a war zone. There was just a mound of stuff where those who wanted to risk their life and sanity could spend time sifting through a pile, as though it was some type of therapeutic exercise. But because everything was lumped together and not planned out in categories and departments, a seemingly simple task (e.g. finding a certain item) was made exponentially more difficult. The same tension between lumping together compared to purposed movement is present when moving your church toward revitalization and health.

Look back to the scriptures that you settled on to be foundational for your church, there can be a desire to just unveil the verse/passage to the congregation and say, "go for it" - to hang up a banner and invite all to join in the journey. But such a move would be akin to the pile of merchandise. Imagine going to the property you just purchased for your home to be built on only to find the contractor had all the supplies piled up by the road with a sign that read "go for it." Imagine the chaos and frustration, and probably failure, that would follow. Instead of the pile, we need order.

What we want to do now is identify some memorable words or phrases that can emerge from your adopted biblical passage, that will give some orderly handles whereby your mission, vision and strategy can come together for your people. (FYI:

Mission – Why you exist; Vision – Where you are going; Strategy – How you are going to get there).

Back to the house construction analogy. A set of plans for one house has several sub-plans – electrical, plumbing, foundation, etc. All of these come together for the overall house. Similarly, biblically rooted words or phrases will serve as missional layers (plans) that will work together to build the biblical vision for your church.

Begin to attach descriptive words that summarize your foundational scripture. For instance, if one of your verses is Matthew 28:19-20, the Great Commission, you might choose words such as "Go" "Share" Reach." If you choose Matthew 21, the Great Commandment, you might choose words such as "Love", "Connect", "Know." (Consider placing "ing" to the end of your word to give the word more action – "loving"). For assistance, look in a thesaurus (yes, they still print those) or see what words come up through alternate translations and other online linguistic tools.

As you are searching for the right word that encapsulates the scripture you have embraced as an anchor for your church, keep all words parallel (ex. lov<u>ing</u>, reach<u>ing</u>, shar<u>ing</u> as opposed to loved, connecting, share). Additionally, notice if your foundational passage(s) has some commonalities you want to join together, and consider using an anchor word that is used in all the phrases to communicate that (ex. serving God, serving the church, serving the world).

Before you or your planning team puts your idea in stone, let it simmer for a bit. Let your team think and pray on it for a week or two. Run it by someone outside the church, a trusted third-party; even consider asking a non-Christian (ex. "We are trying to get clarity about the purpose of our church, can I get your feedback?"). Such a strategy conversation could turn the corner to a gospel conversations. This step will reduce the possibility of adopting a phrase that, while biblically rooted, is confusing to the listener or is actually offensive to the people you are seeking to reach. (I have actually had to contact a church to urgently have them change their marquee because their seemingly cute statement on forgiveness was actually a known vulgar phrase in the community. They had no idea.)

At the end of the movie "A Few Good Men," both Tom Cruise's and Jack Nicholson's character ask, "Am I clear?" Their answer: "crystal." Being crystal clear is imperative when leading toward revitalization. If you don't take the extra time to get to "crystal," those following you will fill in the blanks with their opinion as to what *they think* you are referring to, which may or may not be correct (usually not). It will be imperative that you define your terms, beginning with the scripture you have chosen.

Here's an example:

Loving God: Church, a foundation of our church is "Loving God" based off the Great Commandment. As we embrace loving God, we will be seeking to embody that love in the following three ways.

a) We will show love based on the life of our Savior, Christ Jesus (Sacrificial and not Selfish)

b) *We will show love by placing our faith in Jesus Christ and encouraging others to do the same (He is the ONLY way).*

c) *We will show love by conducting our lives and the activities of this church through the application of the Bible (Sanctification and Service).*

And then continue this process to bring clarity for each of your key phrases. Don't leave the defining of terms to others. The stakes are too high. This is part of discipleship – taking people where they are and building them into the body God desires them to be. The execution of this process doesn't mean those in your church will not have decisions to make for their daily personal lives; rather, you are establishing clear borders that free your people to run around in while still being connected to the overall body of the church.

Once you have the primary phrases in place, which are rooted in the Bible, you now have a blueprint for you to follow for planning and pastoring. Below are some sample questions that can aid in shaping your church in a biblical direction, thus leading toward revitalization and health.

1. *What series do I need to preach that will help our people understand "Loving God" sacrificially?*
2. *How can we plan VBS so that it clearly teaches kids to love God? What will be a way that we can clearly show the love of God to kids in VBS?*
3. *What events did we have last year that did not fulfill our biblical foundation of "Loving God"?*
4. *How can we change our budget so that someone first glancing at it would see our biblical priorities?*

Having this agreed upon biblical blueprint will help ensure everyone is rowing in the same direction. Just as having six people in a boat who are all rowing in slightly different directions will get you nowhere, not to mention very weary and frustrated, having your church all serving towards different self-identified ends can lead to the same aggravating result. Consequently, finances will be wasted, energies will be expended, and relationships will be agitated, all because the focus was not clear – crystal clear.

I spent much of my middle school through college years behind the mouthpiece of a trumpet, playing in marching, concert and jazz bands. From first-hand account I can assure you that the sound is not pleasant when a room filled with even the most skilled of musicians are playing different songs at the same time.

Having agreed upon a biblical framework to follow will help your church play off the same sheet of music – God's word. Additionally, it will also give clarity to your leadership. When people ask, "Why are we attempting this new endeavor?" "We have never done that before." You can easily respond, "We have agreed together as a church that we will fulfill the second Great Commandment to love our neighbor – loving others. Since this ministry opportunity is directly in line with that commandment, even though out of our normal comfort zone, we are pursuing it so to be biblical doers of the word and not hearers only."

The Bible is more than a bunch of *good* stuff. It is *God* stuff. Don't just pile it up for the willing to dive in, present it for all to discover.

Toward Reflection

1. What are key words or phrases that we can articulate from our agreed upon biblical foundation?
2. What order do these words or phrases need to be in?
3. What clarity or definitions do we need to give to each word or phrase?

Toward Revitalization: Where you Are

Prayerful
Biblical
Categorical
Contextual
Directional
Organizational
Functional
Communicative
Evaluative

CHAPTER 5

STEP 4 | CONTEXTUAL

"...having determined their appointed times and the boundaries of their habitation..."
-Acts 17

7.6 Billion people in the world. 327 Million people in the United States alone. Some missiologists estimate the number of churches in the world is approaching 37 million. Billion or million, regardless of your math skills, that is a bunch; however, your church is one of a kind. Though you might be in a city that has a church on every corner, there is only ONE church like yours. Though you might be in a denomination that numbers in the thousands, no other church has *the same* fingerprint as does yours. The Apostle Paul told the people in Athens that God even appointed the times and places when people live (Acts 17). Thus, we are ordained by sovereign God and are here for a purpose. Of all the periods in the history of the world, God has appointed for your church to exist *now*. And of all the places within the expanse of earth, God has appointed for your church to gather in *your* community. Though others might be just up the road, none are identical. None have your God-created DNA. Because of such specialness and purpose, we need to be a steward of our time and place of ministry. It is wise to know your church's fingerprint and foolish to merely copy the methods of another (who are always different from us).

The reason for determining your church's fingerprint is for the application of the Bible. By this point in your journey toward revitalization, your church has established a culture of prayer where you are praying for God to move in your midst, in your personal life, in your church and in your community. Additionally, you have established a biblical foundation for your church with some memorable phrases that provide handles of understanding. Consequently, knowing the "ins and outs" of your present context, the real-time of your community, will be essential if you are to apply what you learn from God's word and for you to lift non-generic prayers (ex. "save John Smith who lives at 4 Elm Street" instead of "save our community").

Discovering your church's context will take work. Research, interviews, honest evaluation and more will take much time and effort. There can be no assuming that you understand the context of your community just because you have been there a long time. Communities change. We are growing more isolated. We tend to move blindly fast through familiar places rather than observe slowly. We tend to be creatures of routine and only view the world through a repeated lens – e.g. watching or reading the same news sources that we agree with. We can live like pod people.

Consequently, many churches find themselves disconnected and diverging from the mission field around them because their community has changed; and the church is still functioning in the way that was relevant years, sometimes decades, in the past. What is more, those days in the past might be viewed as "the good old days" and thus everyone wants to work harder to return to them. But the community is not there in the days long gone. The mission of God is not relegated to back then. The people for whom God purposed for you to influence in the gospel are before and around you. It is imperative that you discover what actually *is* and not make assumptions because of what once was.

How?

Demographic Research

Check with your local denomination's association or state convention for assistance in acquiring demographic research for a radius of 1, 3 or 5 miles out from your church, or specific road borders if possible. You can also gather reports from census.gov (e.x. American Community Survey) and/or inquire of local, city, or county agencies that could provide you with the additional data. When you get the report, look for the average age of your community, the education level, poverty level, the ethnic make-up and the trends of each of these during the past decade as well as future projections.

Interview

Face to face conversations will give you the best results. Identify an agreed upon area surrounding your church. The size of this area will depend on the size of your church. For instance, if you have a church of 100 people, keep your ministry area to a radius of about 1000 people. A 10:1 ratio - community: attender - can be a good starting point. Once you have a good relational grip on that area, then consider expanding. When your area is identified, go door to door in that community conducting a needs survey (limit your survey to no more than 7 questions).

Sample questions:

- What's the biggest need that you see in the community?
- What areas of brokenness do you see in the community?
- If a church were to make an impact in this community, what would they do?

Besides the questions, have the interviewer take additional notes from their observations such as ethnic, age, and culture.

Complete a Panorama[14]

Imagine a window with the various sectional lines. Using the divider lines, your window now has four sections, sections by which you see the community and the community sees you.

- Pane 1: inside church to community – these are questions and answers from your church about how those in your church view your community.

[14] NAMB, "Replant | Associational Guide", (Alpharetta, North American Mission Board, 2018), page 11-12.

- Pane 2: outside church to community – these are questions and answers from your community about how they view your community.
- Pane 3 – inside church to church – these are questions and answers from those in your church about how they view your church.
- Pane 4 – outside church to church – these are questions and answers from individuals in your community about how they view your church.

Your goal is to get as many answers as possible so that you have an accurate window on your community and on your church, and then compare and contrast as to how each sees the other. During this process it might be helpful to lead your people on a tour of the community by conducting a driving observational survey. Have them make notes what needs did they see: what opportunities did they notice, what thoughts would they have if they were touring your community for the first time as a missionary.

When all this data is gathered, you will then have a clear picture of your community (needs, jobs, ethnicity, age). You will also have information about how some in your community view your church. This will be helpful for you, but it might also sting a bit.

Now, before you discredit the opinion of the community "heathen," wait. While you take direction from God and the Bible, the opinion of the community can inform the priority of your steps and give you some starting points on where you should apply biblical truths. Even Paul the Apostle adjusted his approach to sharing the gospel depending on who he was talking to. Further, knowing how those in your church view your context, both inside the church and out in the community, will reveal obstacles and opportunities you might have missed earlier.

Two final suggestions. One, it might help for your people to visualize your community by having a cartoon figure or stock photo of someone up on a wall who represents a norm in your community. Call him "community Carl" or "community Cathy."[15] Then, when you are planning ministry opportunities, keep in mind the uniqueness of "Carl" or "Cathy" based on what you know from your community analysis.

[15] This suggestion is expressed as "Unchurched Harry and Mary" in Rick Warren's *The Purpose-Driven Church.*

Second, it will be helpful for a person who looks like those in your community to have a presence on the platform during your worship gatherings. When guests from your community attend your corporate gatherings and see people in leadership with whom that can relate, they will feel more welcome and sense that your church is a place for them. (Note: These two items will not replace your church being friendly, welcoming and loving to *all* who come.)

Toward Reflection

1. Where will we research to learn present composition and trends of our community?
2. How will we engage our community to better learn who they are today?
3. If Jesus was a member of this team, what would He be doing to know and reach this community?

Toward Revitalization: Where you Are

Prayerful
Biblical
Categorical
Contextual
Directional
Organizational
Functional
Communicative
Evaluative

CHAPTER 6

STEP 5 | DIRECTIONAL

"The mind of man plans his way, But the LORD directs his steps."
– Proverbs 16:9

I have a surprise for you. You already have your mission. Perhaps you have wondered when I was going to urge your team to create a long mission statement. But you already have it. Look back to the foundational passage you selected. This is what you have determined as your mission – why your church exists. (If desired, there are many great resources available that your church can use to craft much more extended mission and vision statements and frameworks. *Church Unique*[16] or *Unstuck*[17] are two great resources I recommend. I encourage you to get them and work through them. They are great resources just outside the scope I have set for this book.)

In this chapter we will order those descriptive phrases or "handles" that will serve as the underpinnings of your strategy. This ordering will guide your people as to what they are to do first, second and so on.

Let's use the fast-food industry to explain further. Pick your favorite fast-food restaurant. Chances are you have eaten at this restaurant across a chain of restaurants – near you, across town, another city or state. Regardless of where you choose to enjoy the culinary experience, the food tastes the same. Why? There is an order of food development by which the owner has trained the employees to follow in order to reach the standard tasty outcome. If the process was

---

[16] Mancini, Will, *Church Unique: How Missional Leaders Cast Vision*, (San Francisco: Josey Bass Publishers, 2008).
[17] Morgan, Tony, *Unstuck: Equipping Church to Experience Sustained Health*, (Nashville: Harper Collins, 2017).

left to the preparer's preference, then the expectation of a certain taste would be in jeopardy and the owner's plan would not be met – this would be a loss of quality control.

This same process must be extended to discipleship. Jesus often remarked, "if you want to be my disciple…" and then He laid out the spiritual ingredients. Perhaps the most frequent comment I hear these days is, "I wish I had a plan to follow so I knew what to do next in my faith." This statement is from new Christians as well as those more seasoned, and across church contexts. In a day where so much of life has a plan for people to follow (even in Bible reading apps), there is a growing demand for church leadership to give first, second, and third steps.

Busyness does not equal godliness. (You have probably heard that one). Likewise, mounding up a pile of rocks does not comprise a clear path to walk on. All too often churches will equate the amount of activity in their church calendar with health. Thus, the more items on the calendar, the better the church. The newsletters are filled with events and meetings, but nothing is connected to why the church exists in the first place. When asked how they are doing, the normal response is, "We are staying quite busy." But such "busyLIFE" thinking, ambition and practice will leave a church far short of the biblical mandate to make disciples[18], to be witnesses both locally and abroad[19], and to be ambassadors of reconciliation between God and man[20]. Sadly, I have seen all too many churches that have busy calendars boast of their activity but are experiencing great decline in health.

Today's fast-paced culture tends to view time as of *greater value* than money; thus, someone will more readily write a check for a worthy cause as opposed to volunteering their time. Why? Their money "costs less" in their eyes than their time. As such, time is viewed as most precious. Jesus said, "For where your treasure is, there will your heart be also" (Matthew 6:21). And with time being so precious, spending time biblically is a matter of discipleship, a matter that church leaders must speak into; and you need to be

---

[18] Matthew 28:19-20

[19] Acts 1:8

[20] 2 Corinthians 5:18-19

prepared to lead them in light of their mindset toward the preciousness of time. Your congregants and your community will look to you to give them clarity as to what an authentic follower of Jesus looks like despite the mixed messages that swirl around them and can compete with biblical living.

Questions your people are asking:

1. How do I live every day with a God-centered life?
2. As I want to grow in my faith, what is the most important part of the church I need to be connected to? What is second?
3. If I am to take the next step of growth as a Christian, what is it? What will it cost me?

Elizabeth was a new Christian I met in the community. Hearing she recently had trusted Jesus as her Savior, I asked her if she had yet found a local church. Her response was alarming, "No, there are just so many I just get confused and don't know what to do; I'll just wait on the church thing." Her large amount of church options had actually paralyzed her from making a decision. Mike was a long-time member in one of the churches I serve. Though he was quite busy in the church-filled calendar, he privately expressed he was unsure what was His next step as a follower of Jesus should be and wished the church would give him clear steps to follow in His relationship with Jesus as opposed to having yet another event to show up to. It's like going into an ice-cream shop and having more than ten flavors and the decision process will nearly paralyze; have three decisions and the speed of decision is much quicker and still with high satisfaction. A pile paralyzes, a path guides.

Similarly, people in your church will be paralyzed in their spiritual development if they are overwhelmed with options and don't have clarity as to the next step they can take. They will see the activities of your church as a pile of religious merchandise that they have to sort their way through instead of well-organized departments or categories they can easily navigate through on the biblical journey of growing in faith. Thus, church leaders should intentionally unstack the pile of ministry rocks, throw some away, and create a clear pathway for the Christ follower to follow.

For instance, the most important action items you desire a person to do is what? Look back to your foundational biblical passage and those categorical phrases you developed. Which of those items is first? In other words, of all the steps or decisions you desire a person to take, which is most important and comes first. For example, a person being a follower of Jesus is of greater importance than them finding a place of ministry. Keep this process up.

My son Elijah has recently begun to golf. A program he has been participating in is called *Operation36*[21]. The purpose is to take the golf newbie and grow him or her in their skills. There are twelve basic skills to work on. Their first challenge is to stand twenty-five yards away from the center of the green, apply their skills and shoot thirty-six or less across nine holes. When they can accomplish this, their same twelve skills increase a little in difficulty and they are moved back to fifty yards away from the green. The

[21] https://operation36.golf

process repeats at 100 yards, 200 yards and then at two sets of tee boxes. In total, there are seventy-two difference objectives – twelve steps that get slightly more difficult across six levels. Thus, the young golfer has a set pathway to follow, under the encouragement and guidance of the coach, to make progress and mature as a player. When I saw this, I saw discipleship all over it – a pathway for the new Christian to grow in their faith under the encouragement and guidance of a biblical mentor. My reaction, if golf has thought through a player's development, shouldn't we as the church think intentionally about a Christian's development?

Take some time and lay out the steps you want your people to walk that would lead them to the outcome you desire. Now that you have your biblical items in an order, a pathway, ensure that everyone knows what that item means. Repeat it, declare it, communicate it, in multiple ways. Additionally, give clarity about the when, where and how that person can engage in that most important item. Do they schedule an appointment, attend a class, get baptized, or take some other first step? Then, after that person has taken that first step, is the direction clear as to the next step they are to take and then the third? And is there clarity about the when, where and how for each of those?

Often churches can assume people know how to get to where the preacher says they are to get. The words are broadcast loudly and frequently (hopefully) – "Be a Disciple of Jesus!" Great. So, what's the first step? The second? The third? If not careful, those who spend all their time in the "bubble" of church, especially if they grew up going to church, will assume everyone knows what to do next when in reality nobody does. Sadly, the failure to articulate will paralyze the new Christian, not get them moving in the preferred direction of spiritual maturity. If these are not articulated, your church will just become a place of non-productive activity where everyone is roaming around like the children of Israel wandering in the desert. They will gauge their spiritual maturity on the number of programmed events they attend instead of how their life is being transformed into Christ-likeness.

Permit me to let you in on a secret that you don't know: the people in your church are frustrated – not necessarily with the content you are giving them; rather, not knowing what to do with it.

Let me add another point. Helping people walk the pathway is best done in the context of a relationship. Sure you can have a class, a sermon series or a handout. Sure you can make a series of videos, banners and billboards. It can even be wise to have set events that are promoted for people at one point to step to another. But the most effective environment will be when one more mature follower of Jesus Christ invests himself or herself in one or two other people who are coming behind them in their faith. They regularly get together to talk about where they are and hold each other accountable for whatever might be next. Could this be slower in the short run? Yes. But it will bring about exponential growth and health in the near future.

I realize that shifting from a ministry "pile" to a "pathway" can be painful. After putting your current ministries under each category, you might discover there is a fond event/program that doesn't fit. Thus, you will have to decide if you keep the long-standing event or ministry for the sake of tradition and comfort (thus sucking additional energy and resources of the church that way) or remove that ministry or event so that you can focus in the direction everyone has agreed you need to go. This process might include removing ministries or events, "pruning" to use a biblical term, in order to experience the fruit you desire.

At this point, look back to the ministry items that you articulated from your adopted biblical texts which you have placed in categories. Now, of those items, What is first? What is second? What is third? Are there steps within each of those? What are they? Make them crystal clear.

Toward Reflection

1. What do we want our people to do first?
   (alt. What is most important?)
2. What is next?
3. Where do we need to be clearer on our pathway to maturity?

Toward Revitalization: Where you Are

Prayerful

Biblical

Categorical

Contextual

Directional

Organizational

Functional

Communicative

Evaluative

CHAPTER 7

STEP 6 | ORGANIZATIONAL

"Everything should be done in a fitting and orderly way."

– 1 Corinthians 14:40

What got you here won't get you there. Besides this being the title of a great book by Marshall Goldsmith, it is also an essential principle to remember as your church is seeking to move toward revitalization. For instance, the organization of your church (e.g. organizational structure, role of staff, function of committees, guiding documents) were probably assembled at some point far back in your church's history, in our nation's history. Your committees were assembled accordingly because of some denominational standard, and your staffing was assembled as accustomed for all churches at that particular moment in time. But the context of your church and community has changed since that organization was put in place.

Consider your community for just a moment. From discovering the details of your context (chapter 5), has there been changes in your community from what it *was* ten or twenty years ago? Have moral norms changed? Has the complexity of schedules increased – more to do, more options competing for the same amount of time, more information that exposes us to…more? Different? Your community has definitely changed though you might feel more resistant to admit your church has changed. Days of yesteryear are not the days of today.

However, when comparing your church to some point in the past, decline occurred (refer back to chapter 1). That gap, big or small, between the mission field of your community and the current reality of your church is much different. Though your biblical mission must be forever connected to the word of God, how your church is currently organized is likely disconnected from how God wants your church to fulfill that mission moving forward. Change is needed.

Now, let me take a pause and clarify something – by "change" I am *not* referring to biblical truths. I am *not* referring to theology. I *am* referring to methodology. The Bible does not change, and we must not change it in order to "be relevant." However, the methodology which we use to deliver the unchanging word of God must change. We cannot confuse theology and methodology.

For example, in the 21st century the Biblical text is not confined to be delivered solely through print; now the Bible is able to be transmitted digitally. Thus, the content (the Bible) did not change, but the method (print to digital) did. This shift (who are we kidding, "change") in transmitting the gospel can be akin to the change from the *handwritten* scroll handled only by the priest to the *machine printed* biblical text available to the masses. Again, the content (the Bible) did not change but the method (print to digital) did.

I am observing, sadly, church after church who confuse this matter and contend that *both* methodology and theology are of equal importance, even equal sacredness. Such churches are, seemingly, as willing to take a bullet for long-held practices and policies as readily as they are for biblical dogma. That is flawed. Our contextual and historical methods in and of themselves are neither inerrant nor infallible. They are not immutable like the character of God or the word of God. For example, the presence of a flower committee to ensure which arrangement is on the Lord's Supper table each week is not of equal value as the gospel that articulates how one can be reconciled back to God. Having three different administratively focused committees instead of one is not of equal worth as "be my witnesses…to the end of the earth" (Acts 1:8). The front row completion of a response card at the end of a service is not *the only way* to confess one's faith before men and God.

As an Associational Missional Strategist, I see such confusion on a regular basis. At times there is a great passion to preserve the methodology yet apathy on the theology. I walk into a church and feel I have walked through a time warp. The church seems to have hit the "pause" button in a particular decade and held up certain cherished methods as most sacred by their actions; or rather, inaction. (More on that in the next chapter.) The church seeking to move toward revitalization and health must ensure that a presently effective, yet biblically-sound, organization is in place that will assist the church in moving toward their preferred future.

Take a moment to consider where I have placed this topic on organization. Consider the topics that we have already covered and have been building upon: *After* much prayer. *After* biblical investigation. *After* the context of the present mission field has been investigated. *After* the kingdom pathway has been laid. The reason? The church moving toward revitalization and health must gain the big picture of where they feel God taking them before constructing an organization to help them get there. If this process is reversed, the question will be, "What can we get done with the organization we currently have?"; not, "Where is GOD leading us and what organization do we need in order to get there?" Notice the driver. The former starts with us and the latter starts with God.

Unhealthy churches gain their marching orders based off their bylaws, policies and church history. Healthy churches determine their steps from the Bible as they walk in the present day with the Holy Spirit. Unhealthy churches primarily look back to former peaks of ministry when God moved. Healthy churches prayerfully look for the next opportunity for God to move. Unhealthy churches cry out loudest for everyone to follow Robert's Rules of Order. Healthy churches cry out loudest for everyone to follow the Bible.

Now, don't think that I am against order and guidelines and bylaws and policy. One of my favorite verses is 1 Corinthians 14:40, "Everything should be done in a fitting and orderly way." I routinely help churches write organizational documents and am happy to do so. I am often referred to as the "admin nerd." I have read scores of books on order and polity, and I think that healthy churches should have healthy policies that they follow. However, too many churches give higher value and credence to their organizational documents than their biblical mandates – perhaps not verbally but in practice. With that out of the way, let's get some organizational elements knocked out.

Statement of Belief

Establish a crystal clear statement of belief that encompasses what your church believes. This statement will be a reference point for numerous other organizational aspects (e.g. membership, wedding guidelines, facility usage, moral statements, and much more.) When articulating your Statement of Belief, be crystal clear. Words have meaning, and you need to determine what those words mean. In our day of rapidly changing morals, words are being twisted. Don't leave room for this abuse and verbal perversion.

Structure

Develop a church structure that assists your church in accomplishing its stated mission. Begin with a blank sheet of paper and make a relevant structure, while remaining biblical of course, instead of trying to prop up an old and irrelevant older one. The structure will include both staff (paid and volunteer) and ministry teams/committees. Note: getting outside help at this point will be greatly helpful so that emotional affections to old forms will not trump a biblical future. As you are putting your structure together, specifically your teams/committees, keep the administration of the church lean and stream-lined. Thus, more people should be participating in carrying out the mission of the church than administrating the organization. It doesn't make sense for 80% of your people to be serving in admin areas thus leaving the work of gospel ministry to the pastor, staff, and the few. Big idea: if more people are working on the ministry than in it, your church will not experience the revitalization and health it desires. Example: Instead of having numerous administrative committees (e.g. finance, personnel, bylaws, education/mission, etc.), have one. Whatever structure you land on, accountability and quality must not be diminished, but more people should be deployed to fulfill the biblical mission instead of greasing organizational cogs.

Policies

Now that your biblical foundation is in place, you know your current community context, and your people are praying, what policies need to be in place so that everyone will be working off the same page? Three points to note:

1. Your guidelines should be connected to your statement of beliefs. The guidelines your church establishes should not keep people moored to preference, rather it should keep them moored to scripture.
2. Your guidelines should be as short as possible. We have the Holy Spirit to guide into all truth; thus, we should not feel the need to write down the actions for every case we can imagine. Set big biblical boundaries and move on.

3. Actually follow your policies. Say what you are going to do and do what you say. The church cannot write policies that will guide their actions and then shelve them except under crisis.

These three points will free your church to move forward at a biblically focused and missionally flexible pace. Tony Morgan, church revitalization author and speaker, has often said, "Why should a church be set up for everyone to say 'no' but no one to say 'yes.'"

Moving from current policies to needed policies could require minor edits, major overhauls, or even scrapping the former all together and replacing them. If you think such a change is impossible, perhaps you need to consider if your church holds a confusion between methodology and theology?

Finances

If I were to pick up a copy of your church's annual budget (which you should have), could I clearly see the mission, vision and values of your church? Further, if I were to review your monthly and/or year-to-date report, would I see that you have conducted yourself according to what you have indicated is important. The way we use our money is a reflection of what we value. "Where our treasure is, there our heart will be also" (Matthew 6:21). This means the way you spend your money must be in line with what you say is your purpose. And "we've always spent money this way in the past" is not a justification for future behavior.

The changes that have been described above are big. Depending on the church they can feel down-right devastating. Thus, the speed by which you make such changes should be carefully monitored. The degree of unhealth will determine your speed. The degree by which your church feels its current pains will determine how you get from where you are to where you need to be. The amount of trust that your church has in those who are leading the change is crucial. Thus, as you are changing the organization of your church to move toward revitalization, focus on *how* you get there and not just *where* you are going.

Toward Reflection

1. What is our statement of belief? How can we incorporate that statement into our daily function and guiding documents?
2. What should the structure of our church look like that would aid us in reaching our preferred future?
3. What financial adjustments need to occur so that our treasures reflect our mission?

Toward Revitalization: Where you Are

Prayerful
Biblical
Categorical
Contextual
Directional
Organizational
Functional
Communicative
Evaluative

CHAPTER 8

STEP 7 | FUNCTIONAL

Walk according to the calling by which you have been called."

– Ephesians 4:1

One of my favorite educational tools I gleaned from regularly growing up was Schoolhouse Rock. In their doctoral level curriculum (my personal opinion), "conjunction junction" was a staple. The grammar-based train depot helped me to hook up words and phrases and clauses. But do you remember the main phrase? "Conjunction Junction what's your function?" (Everybody sing!)

Like in grammar, a church moving toward revitalization must have a "conjunction junction" that moves it toward the practical function of the church. It hooks up the ideals, mission and values with the behaviors of the every day. If basic functions of the church are skipped, the church will never gain the traction it needs to put desire into outcomes. The proclamations will only be ideals that inform not guide and direct.

The functional aspect of a church moving toward revitalization is often overlooked. In this chapter I am referring to the tangible aspects of ongoing ministry - building, bills, budgets. The functional step of ministry.

Building

Buildings are tools God uses for His glory – to both grow His people and to reach more people. While a building is not required to be a healthy New Testament church, they can be tools to aid in the process. But they can also be a hindrance. If not managed well, buildings can become like untamed vines that actually impede God's desires instead of assist. To ensure your building is helping you move toward revitalization, review the function of your facility according to the items below.

Clean Out the Clutter

Rooms should not be filled with outdated material, broken items and unnecessary resources. If there is ANY room in your church that contains such items, they should be tossed. Rent a dumpster, or two, and begin cleaning. Could this mean that some items might be tossed that are connected to fond memories? Yes. But the mission of God that remains for the future of your church is of greater Kingdom value than the item from your past. If your church has a greater desire to use a room to store old items than to use the same room to disciple new Christians, you don't have a storage issue, you have a heart issue. Expose that. Thus, clean out the clutter and prepare yourselves, without and within, for the next task God has laid on your heart.

Clean in General

The facility needs to communicate you were expecting guests to arrive and you love the members who invest their time and resources. Further, your facility needs to communicate that God is worthy of our very best, where we give Him excellence in our lives and in the tools that He entrusts to us. I have attended a countless number of churches where mold and grime are growing on the sides of their building – literally deep black and dark green. If asked, I would have been hesitant to answer the intended color of the building. (Like sin – it can grow slowly and sometimes unnoticed). Consider, what glory to God does an unkept church give? What message about the relevance of God in our everyday life does broken gutters and flaking paint give to those who drive by and/or live near your church campus. While the people who comprise the church may exude a deep love for God, a friendly and Christ-like disposition and who eagerly share their faith with all who they engage, the facility that people see first, *before* they meet the great people within, will give a different and the first impression – and you will have to overcome it. If this is a big undertaking for your church, start small and stick with it. You never get a second chance to make a first impression.[22]

Design

Align the space to the purpose or outcome you desire to have occur within that space. For instance, if your church desires for life connection and discipleship to occur in a given space, ensure the room is set up for that purpose – sitting in rows facing forward won't cut it. If you want relationships to be fostered within a given space, what colors and furniture would aid that purpose (think relational environment of a coffeehouse versus speedy-service of a fast food restaurant). If you want information given out without much dialogue (more like a master/teacher/lecture format), ensure white-boards

[22] Don't be afraid to ask for help from other churches if the cleaning project is too overwhelming.

and tables are present. Further, consider *who* will be in the room – senior adult ladies or middle school boys. And then establish your room with *them* in mind. I find it humorous, yet also sad, when churches are confused as to why young people don't come back when the entire environment communicates "we were not expecting *you*."

Further, realize that codes and building norms change overtime. Having a campus that is friendly to those with disabilities will be essential to minister to those in your community. As an Associational Missional Strategist who is in a different church nearly every week, I was told by a couple that when they were looking for a church, they really liked another church but were unable to get in and out of that facility; thus, they chose a different church. Additionally, there are much higher expectations on security and child safety in the American culture. These were not primary issues when most church facilities were constructed and perhaps even when ministry furniture was purchased. For better and for worse, people who are exploring church and contemplating the Christian faith are often making their decision on how well you take care of them while on campus.

Remember, a growing number of people in our community have NEVER been in a church facility apart from a wedding or a funeral. Further, fear is a major driver for decision making in our culture today. Though we have not been given a spirit of fear[23], those who are new to your church and still disconnected from a relationship with God don't have the peace of God within them yet – we are hoping to get them there. Thus, while God is working on the inside of the person, we need to be simultaneously thinking about them on the outside as well. I don't mean we have metal detectors at the entrance and retinal scanners when picking up the child from the nursery, but properly public and appropriately discreet systems need to be in place.

Signage

[23] 2 Timothy 1:7

Having proper signage around your campus is also essential. We'll cover that more in the next chapter.

Bills

This is a functional component that has to do with the money. Churches are being asked to do more with less. Further, there are so many headlines telling of financial abuse within the church or a Christian organization. Consequently, ensuring how your money fulfills your mission/vision according to your strategy is of paramount importance. Let's consider some actions you can take.

Balanced with Bank

Are you confident that the records of your church are in alignment with what is indicated in your financial institutions? Is the report that is given you and the church identical to the bank? If not, you need to find out why. Remember, those resources don't belong to you (or really even belong to the church). They belong to God, and you must be a good steward of His resources – of which you will give an accounting for one day. Further, giving evidence that you are in alignment with the bank can be a great word of confidence to guests and members alike by communicating that your church is a place that can be trusted and where more of their lives and resources can be invested.

Itemized Review

Bills can serve to create a check-list for areas to investigate and possibly improve. For instance, when the phone bill comes you can check to see if you are getting the best rate or if a different phone system could better serve your current needs. When the power bill comes, check to see if adjustments are possible to your meter, insulation, windows or other places where energy efficiency is lost. Often contracts can be renegotiated, or rebates are available. New technology can also save time and money in the long run. Could this mean breaking ties with a company who has provided a certain service for decades? Yes. But you will have to decide as to what is more important - the business relationship with a company (that might cost more and may offer less) or going a new route that could free up resources to reach the lost or hungry or needy around you.

Sound Practices

Having sound financial practices are of paramount importance. With America being such a litigious society, one allegation of impropriety can be catastrophic to a church. Keeping signed checks tucked away in the secretary's desk is not wise. Having Deacon Smith take the offering home after church and then to the bank on his way to the office on Monday is giving an open door for Satan and evil to walk through. Entrusting one person to count the offering, deposit the contributions, cut and sign checks, and report to the church, without oversight or accountability, is mounting up tremendous risk on the individual and the church. (Personally, "red flags" go up if a person demands sole control of finances and refuses accountability or to share the responsibility). Making adjustments so that your church reflects wise accounting practices will produce dividends in both the short term and long term.

Budgets

How you spend your money is a reflection of what you truly believe. Further, how you *plan* to spend your money will serve as a road map to fulfill the missional strategy you have set toward revitalization. Someone glancing at your budget document should easily be able to see your purpose. Thus, consider some of the following questions when forming your budget.

1. **Prayer**: How has prayer shaped our hearts when preparing for the financial future of our church?
2. **Give**: What has God laid on our hearts to give to partner organizations to exponentially increase the mission God has given us (example: Cooperative Program = 10% of undesignated funds; Local Association = 2% of undesignated funds; International Mission Board = 1% of undesignated funds; North

American Mission Board (Annie Armstrong) = 1% of undesignated funds)?[24]

3. **Operations**: What obligations do we have to ensure we have an effective ministry tool in our facility (ex. insurance, power, utilities, repair and maintenance)? Are we getting the best rates/deals at each business?
4. **Savings**: Are we prepared in our savings account should an emergency cause us to miss receiving an offering for a week or a month? Have we saved a significant amount of money over a period of time that is only for "a rainy day" but has no stated plan and could be redirected toward Kingdom impact?
5. **Ministry**: What has God called us to do as a church? How will our budget aid us in that calling?
6. **Staff**: Are we properly taking care of the pastors God has called to equip and lead our church? There are numerous guides and

[24] Recommendation: If churches incorporate the annual special offerings into their regular giving plan, they can celebrate what they have *already* given and not only ask for more when a particular season comes around.

booklets that are available for your finance team and/or staff to use to ensure you are operating in a "fitting and orderly way" (1 Corinthians 14:40). Use them.

Have a trusted someone from the outside review your process and budget and welcome them to coach and consult. There is wisdom in many advisors.

Buildings, bills and budget. They sound so mundane. They feel far removed from making disciples of all nations. But these very items are both aids and obstacles for you seeing the health of your church realized. Additionally, permitting spiritually immature individuals to oversee such areas of your church because the tasks don't appear "ministry" in nature will hurt you. So many leaders are longing for momentum when moving toward health. The big "MO." To get the train of momentum moving in your prayer-led direction, don't neglect these areas. Remember, in conjunction junction, function matters.

Toward Reflection

1. How can we adjust our facility so that it is a better tool for the ministry God has called us to today?
2. What bills can we review that could realign our expenditures in order to maximize the kingdom?
3. What changes can we make to our budget that would be a financial plan moving us toward our preferred future?

Toward Revitalization: Where you Are

Prayerful
Biblical
Categorical
Contextual
Directional
Organizational
Functional
Communicative
Evaluative

CHAPTER 9

STEP 8 | COMMUNICATIVE

6 Let your speech always be [a]with grace, as though seasoned with salt.
-Colossians 4:6

Not long ago I was in New York City for a meeting. This was my second time to the Big Apple, both times needing to traverse much of Manhattan to get to my various appointments and desired destinations. Needless to say, I did not know the streets and landmarks like the back of my hand. Which way to turn? Which Metro stop to get off? When can I walk without getting pulverized by a taxi or the pedestrian masses? Fortunately, everywhere I looked were signs. Signs. More signs. Signs advertising products. Signs giving direction. Signs offering deals. Signs begging for donations. And if that mass of messages was not sufficient, nearly everyone around me was on their smartphones voraciously consuming even more.

Communication in the 21st century culture, or at least the *attempt* to communicate, is at a fever pitch. Everyone walks around with their own handheld microphone (their smartphone) and blasts messages through their personalized advertising company (social media). When this amount of communication is multiplied by the millions of participants, simple messages can quickly become background noise. If not careful, the valuable eternal messages of the church can be muted by the empty messages of society; and the people you seek to lead, influence and disciple will be left wandering. Thus, alignment, clarity, and repetition are essential for each church.

Alignment:

Misalignment in your car can cause unnecessary wear and tear; misalignment in your church results in the same. By "alignment" I am referring to the agreement between *what* you believe, what you *say* you believe, and how you *behave* according to what you believe - the agreement between belief, speech, behavior. As I have had the privilege of being in a different church nearly every Sunday, I have observed that churches with a higher level of alignment are generally in better health. None of them are perfect; however, there is intentionality across all the ministries of the church to pursue alignment within themselves and within the church as a whole. Belief, Speech, Behavior.

For alignment to begin, considerable time and energy must be spent on defining as a church what you believe. This is partially covered in the biblical step (chapter 3 and chapter 6) when I urge a clear statement of belief. No longer can a church merely and undefinably say, "we believe the Bible" (Oh, how I wish) because eisegesis and the perversion of scripture is rampant. Like a championship football coach leaves nothing to chance, a good church leader leaves nothing to guess for people pursuing Christ.

After the church has embraced a unified theology, it is time to clearly communicate that belief. Now, I am not suggesting there needs to be a billboard articulating your beliefs when guests pull in the parking lot or painted on the side of your worship center, but why you exist (mission), where you are going as a church (vision) and the process to get there (strategy) should be readily visible from multiple points within the facility…and a bit outside (though the people themselves serve as the best billboard for communication).

Finally, the way your church behaves must be in agreement with what you believe and what you say. For instance, if your church believes the Bible, preaches that it believes the Bible, but the final authority is some policy from thirty years ago, you have misalignment. If you *believe* God wants you to pass your faith on to the future generation, if you *say* you want people of all ages to gather together and worship, but if you *behave* in a way where one generation has preferential treatment over another, there is misalignment. If you believe in the guiding power of the Holy Spirit, if you say you are seeking the face of God through prayer with the help of the Holy Spirit but cave when a couple of people with influential pockets dictate your decisions, there is misalignment. People don't follow what you say, they follow what you do.

Clarity

As mentioned earlier, crystal-like clarity is imperative. The gap between the written word and mental understanding seems to be an ever-widening gap. You cannot simply hang up a banner that states your mission and think everyone who reads it will draw the same conclusion – or if they do will it be the biblical conclusion you desire? Words have meaning.

On Campus

The meaning of those words will ultimately lead to a certain behavior. For instance, take the word "disciple" for a moment. Many churches have embraced a goal that they want to develop "fully-devoted disciples of Jesus." But does everyone know what that looks like? What fruit would be evident in someone who is "fully devoted?" What character qualities are found within a disciple?

If terms are not defined, then everyone will be left to come up with their own definition leading to a very individualistic church. Bringing clarity will move your pastor from shepherding a bunch of sheep to shepherding a flock. One more point on this: when sharing key information that you want your people to embrace, don't rely too much on a bulletin board post. Very few people are taking the time to stop, read and consume the information. At best, 5% of your people will spend thirty seconds at most reading your bulletin board (out of 168 hours in a week with 10's of 1000's of messages before their eyes every day).

To the Public

Clarity in communication must come in the signs that are used outside the campus – campus signs, billboards, etc. It is easy for a church to forget that non-Christians view words differently than those within the church. In growing measure, even in the Bible belt of the South, the community doesn't have a biblical story to process words through. Thus, long-held Christian phrases can be confusing. For instance, imagine driving by a house of worship where you are completely unfamiliar with the basics of their faith - of a different religion all together. Now, imagine reading a marquee that reads "Come get washed in his blood this Sunday at 11 a.m." Operating from a lifelong Christian narrative, I fully understand what that means, but would a non-Christian driving by without any explanation? I am not suggesting that the church abandon theological phrases and connected terminology, but remember who your reader is and define them.

Clarity is also needed as you traverse your campus, regardless of the size of your church. Though you might have been at the church for decades, perhaps even built the building with your own hands, guests have *never* been there. They won't know the difference between the side entrance that everyone uses and the entrance that faces the road (though remains locked). They don't know where the office is compared to the nursery. Thus, in addition to well-placed volunteers in the parking lot and building who are welcoming everyone to a scheduled event and guiding them accordingly, signage needs to be consistent in design and convenient in location and clear in message. Your campus should not be an environment where guests would be like the Children of Israel and wander around lost for 40 years; don't give people a reason to roam. Be clear.

Repetition

Preaching professors often encourage their students to use the following pattern: tell them what you *will* tell them, tell them, tell them what you *already* told them. In a nutshell, repeat and repeat often. In today's high communication culture, important messages can be easily lost. Thus, it is imperative that your leadership identify how you plan to communicate and then be consistent in maximizing those platforms.

Once you have identified those communication platforms (e.g. Facebook, Newsletter, Text, Instagram, Bulletin), the information must be the same in each and the information must be shared over and over again. ONE email or ONE post will not suffice. Additionally, remember that most people connect better to a message that is visual verses text. Thus, a picture or video will go further than a document or other written text. Having a family of icons for the different ministries of your church communicates that the various parts of the church body are still connected and working together. Saying the same thing but from different approaches will keep your content fresh and more people engaged. Let me give you a popular example - changing your church marquee. I have seen numerous churches that keep the content on their sign the same year-round; consequently, my brain doesn't engage because I already know what it says. Subsequently, the message it sends to observers is that what is going on inside the church doesn't change because nothing is changing on the outside. Conversely, a church that keeps their exterior signage fresh communicates that the message on the interior is also fresh. Like it or not, perception is viewed as reality.

Effective communication is a challenge. It will wear you out. It is a task that must be shared with others. Now, regardless of how much you share and how clear you share, some people will remain oblivious. That's life. Just be ready for that as a leader. But don't give them ammunition for the accusation because you have failed to communicate, or you were assuming everyone understood. And if your church still has a way to go to be good at communicating what you desire, God can still work. Thankfully, according to Romans 10:16-21, The Holy Spirit speaks to people from within regardless of the signage that we post without.

Toward Reflection

1. What words are we using that need defining or clarifying?
2. Where can we communicate in a more consistent, convenient and clear manner?

3. What do we need to repeat and how will we go about repeating routinely?

Toward Revitalization: Where you Are

Prayerful
Biblical
Categorical
Contextual
Directional
Organizational
Functional
Communicative
Evaluative

Chapter 10

STEP 9 | EVALUATIVE

"I have glorified you by completing the work you have given Me to do."

– Jesus (John 17:4)

"You staying busy?" Candace and I were out at a nearby restaurant when we ran into someone we have not seen in a little over a year. Her introductory question of "You staying busy?" stuck with me for a long time after the thirty second interaction. Staying busy. Is that the goal? Is that what everyone is pursuing? As opposed to boredom, I guess. This wasn't the first time I have heard this opening question. In pastor social circles I have been asked the same question. But the answer of merely a "yes" or "not really" rings hollow. I have met a lot of busy people who rush to and fro' in a seemingly overdrive of busyness yet have nothing of value to show for it.

Two key questions every church, personally and corporately, must ask in regard to the mission of the church: "What's business?" and "How's business?" In the earlier chapters I have sought to give you a pathway that can lead you to answer for your church the "What's business?" question. Clarity on the biblical foundation, pathways to help you get there, along with contextual, directional, organizational, functional, and communicative steps will help to help foster a better framework that will move your church toward revitalization.

But the second question of "How's business?" is of equal value. It is a question that must be constantly asked. If not, you will just fill your calendar with new items of business and become disconnected from your biblical mandates once again.

I get that gleaning measurable outcomes in all sectors of the church is impossible. God will gauge us according to our faithfulness toward the mission he has given us while He is in charge of the results. Consequently, faithfulness doesn't show up well on a graph. However, there are tools we can put in place to ensure we are giving 100% of our potential faithfulness. Thus, we can humbly present ourselves before God and testify that we did our absolute best, over the long haul, without excuses, with what He has given us. To get to that point, evaluating how we are doing to identify areas to align, adjust and improve will be helpful.

In this chapter I primarily want to supply a bunch of questions that can serve your church to answer the "How's business" question. To help, I'll use the previous chapters as a guide.

How we Got Here

1. Are there any current behaviors and attitudes that reflect the culture we had when our church was in decline?
2. What does our data tell us about ourselves from the last five years? (attendance in worship, small

group, baptisms, giving, per capita giving, average age, baptisms, number of gospel conversations, second time guests, business meeting minutes)?

3. Who could we request to meet with that would be willing to show us our blind spots?

Prayer

1. Can we honestly say we are a "house of prayer?" Would Jesus agree? Would our community?
2. Are we seeing answered prayers in increasing measure?
3. How has participation in prayer opportunities increased or decreased in the last five years?

Biblical & Categorical

1. Are we still centering our church around the same Bible passage? (Ask 5 people who have been at your church under 6 months to help you answer this question).
2. If the answer to number 1 is "no," is there another passage that has replaced it through

the natural course of our ministry practice? If so, which steps do we need to take to further elevate that passage and not send mixed messages?

3. What clarity, crystal-like clarity, do we need to give to our biblical foundation that we didn't see 5 years ago (e.g. defining the terms)? Are our categories clearly reflecting our biblical foundation?

Directional

1. What are the steps toward personal spiritual health and corporate church health that we have established (e.g. our pathway)?
2. Does everyone understand this pathway? (Ask 5 people who have been at your church under 6 months to help you answer this question).
3. If the answer is "no", which step(s), need the most work?

Contextual

1. What do the demographics tell us about the changes in our community (city, county) over the last five years?
2. Does our leadership and our congregation better reflect the makeup of our community than it did 5 years ago?
3. Do our ministries, what is offered and when, match the current reality of our context (alt. - are we adjusting our methodologies to our context or are we expecting our context to adjust to our preferred methodology?)
4. Who are we partnering with to better serve the mission field around us?

Organizational

1. Is our current structure helping us accomplish our biblical mission?
2. Do our current staff positions and the people who are serving them lead and equip the church well toward our preferred biblical future?
3. What ministries or committees need to be stopped or overhauled?

4. Where are we trying to protect past traditions over working toward God's plan for the future?

Functional

1. What part of our campus, inside or out, needs the most attention? Which area is outdated?
2. Is every space of our campus properly set up for its stated purpose?
3. What changes do we need to be evaluated by outside experts so that we are using the resources of our church most wisely (ex. power and/or gas company, insurance, transportation, safety)?

Communicative

1. How healthy is the flow of communication (print, digital)?
2. What communication platforms need to be removed? Need to be added?
3. Who can we ask from both inside and outside the church that will evaluate how we are communicating?

Toward Revitalization: Where you Are

Prayerful
Biblical
Categorical
Contextual
Directional
Organizational
Functional
Communicative
EVALUATIVE

CONCLUSION

Are you a bit overwhelmed at this point? Has all that needs to be considered on the journey toward revitalization seemed a bit complicated? Let me boil it all down in these final sentences.

1. Pray.
2. Dive into the Bible and fall in love with it.
3. Apply God's word into every facet of your church and the mission field that is around you.

Do that faithfully, consistently, and passionately, and the healthy church you desire to see will be realized. The pages you have just waded through simply set an orderly progression for you to consider each and every facet. Above all, be a praying church that stands on and lives out the word of God; and the Holy Spirit who guides us into all truth will illuminate your steps toward revitalization.

ABOUT THE AUTHOR

Brian serves as the Executive Director (Associational Mission Strategist) for the Pensacola Bay Baptist Association (Escambia County, Florida). He is a graduate of University of Mobile ('98) and New Orleans Baptist Theological Seminary ('02, '08). Brian has served local churches in vocational ministry for more than 25 years. He and his wife Candace are natives of Pensacola and have two children, Baleigh and Elijah

Made in the USA
Lexington, KY
16 November 2019

56903795R00068